AF327030

Kid Nigredo

KID NIGREDO

poems by

PHILIP SUNTREE

TURKEY PRESS
1978

Some of these poems have previously appeared in *The Mendocino Grapevine, Kuksu, Beatitudes, Bombast, & The Western Slopes Connection.*

This project was supported, in part, by a grant from the National Endowment for the Arts, in Washington, D. C., a federal agency.

ISBN   0-918824-12-5

Copyright © 1978 by Philip Suntree.
All rights reserved.

for PHYLLIS
my twin sister

TABLE OF CONTENTS

A Note On The Nigredo

The nigredo *is the initial state, either present from the beginning as a quality of the* prima materia, *the chaos, or else produced by the separation of the elements. The* nigredo *is a precise illustration of the initial state of the soul before embarking upon its path of evolution.*

C. G. Jung

Reach inside
can't fly another step
find nothing
where my self runs out
pray so hard
hands hurt
dark
in this body
where the work begins.

HIROSHIMA BABY

Alive in this
my birthday present cloud
the storm Earth could not make,
Earthmaker
here's the smoke
I'm born in bony fear
my Age's dragon speech
says,
Kid
surrender
a warchild believes in rock
prays for wings
claws
anyway to sing the land in meat.

I am this kid of a darkness
suckled on light

as light at evening
slips from the western rim
what is within slips also without

no difference!

Like a shawl in rough hands
my solitude clings
opening the space that is last to die.

My monkey jacket survival kit
sweeping the abandoned dance floor

lunar emptiness
my suit's dark symphonies
slipping silver
between women who speak
as though the horses were waiting

their hands on white tablecloths
and me a child
sleepwalking downstairs to see a fire.

Here's our child adventurer
  the dark mind
  we swim if a day's muscle lets us in
the world's edge
    we touch
          things brightly gathered
    void's terrible wink
  birthing us afraid
  to wake ecstatic memory
lost in the King of Word's arrival.

It takes only one Sun

to slip past the claws the teeth and the hair

where fate, screw-wormed in its apple

floats from arms of the Bear

to squirm through this crack of melted snow

into everything awakened in bones

this path on my two legged walk

with its thirst

that my teeth were not honed

my claws relentlessly sharp

and my own ragged coat amazed by some star

here where I slouch into town

swiping at trees and invisible words

picking their light from my honey-bent tongue.

THE CATCHING

There was always the outside
and the inside
a sea
I think the sea has
as many escapes and fishes
as my lips
years my belly
grew to be a safe
a safe with tumblers
fear hid there
and only fingers remember doors
openings from other hands
touched me
unafraid to leap into a tree
and sing the voice
whose leaves cannot be silent
there are other descriptions
I can steal,
so much to catch
the Sun's a net for any day
opening its mouth
inviting friends
to share my native room.

The sea comes to the cliffs
lips of a breathless giant
my horse shudders
the edge trickles in my spine
calmed by motion
silken as pubic fur
a face upon buttered waters
the Sun's unblinking
yellowed air
a planetary wound
our crazy horse of knowing silence.

Picked her out by curiosity
miles ago
made some promises
kept the night she removed
those clouds
the effulgent foil of undress
tumbling so far
her ancient labor spoke
of course her breast
of course her thigh
of course our lives unspoken
there in the bedroom
at the bottom of the world
we made our dance
and what changed hands
pricelessly the doors swing wide
a moon sits starkly sorrowful
to miss the hesitation of our kiss.

Her crow's foot story
coast by coast
her laughing
            bird eyes
        wings tearing holes in air
    her soft speaking lips
        tracing strange waters over my skin.

What will unleash her, fiery
walking as willow whips
ten thousand green tongues,
when will the furl of her sashay
lick at my calves
and a moon through an oak
shatter night's shade
casting huge antlers on the moon.

OIL

The wife lies
  on her back
  lives open
to their nightly drilling
after years
        she is a land
    gashed, denuded
  of trees, birds, fish,
  her husband
      sees her surface veins
      bleat silence
        a life
he measures in barrels
as in greased silence
      he slaves
      hypnotized
by their own blood pumping
          pumping
              pumping.

CATCHING UP WITH CALAMITY JANE

for Alta

Calamity, to be your Hickok
I could never grow hair long enough
I keep quick hands around each hip
pack a one eye squint
mean new moon
to slip through darkness pale and cold
until loneliness
ushered me these arms
I was cutout a fearful drifter
that sullen loom of shadow woven airs.

On clear nights, running against the dark
muttering crazy music
a carpet of pine needles for wings

feet don't leave the ground
my eyes swallow darkness whole
the instant

I scare up a thought
an ankle catches a stump
the body skids down a clay bank

on hands and knees
wrestling a manzanita thicket
trailing circles round myself

the deer don't give a damn
flicking their ears
standing stifflegged in the leaves.

HAYING

Shattering looseness of light in hay
musk of the new moon
a pitchfork pierces
tish tish
tines slip sunburnt iron
the squat stack settles
burrheaded sheaves
legs brace on stubble
eaves for the rick
wrestled, whu-ay
hup hup a whattizzz
skypulse, hayquill jab
jab — here's your mind
see our unweaving frayed basket
bones and summer thunder
wing of these arms harvesting

One afternoon my work became
a hunchbacked bull
behind the fence
concertina browed
I rode the planets
bulging from that Brahma's eye
flinched at crazy tics
leapfrogging his hide,
inside the chute
he anchored stringy spit to dust
and took a crowfoot stance
lowering puppetbones on his back
scrambling centrifuge
for half-awakened lives
packed my mouth
with bitter gums of dirt
distant cowhand laughter
raised me starry
dazed as any bull-dancer thrown
through the crescent moon.

Feeling luck's arrival
like riding to the mailbox
to pick up a letter written to myself.

At Doc's barn, heavy lidded horses droop
warts and fetlocks shuddering

my only silver settles
snake back cards are taken up
by enchanted squinting gamblers:

flush.

THE GREENMAN

Roots

seek cracks in my mirror

quicksilver flakes

a body

a tree

a fistful of weeds

sharing the fire

in my last lump of coal

vines grapple

arms loop toward light

drift in small green rooms

bandaging the memory of trees.

Our holy slow train flashes silverblue
  lapiz lazuli on flat brown land
a lady in high velvet knows
  what precious stone to hide
so much hidden by trinkety love
  shades a witch where an angel stands

at whistle stops I offer all my teeth
  a coyote smile of absolute belief
pale sleepless swans her lifted hands
  "lapis lazuli does no harm," she smiled
our holy slow train takes its arc
  stretching West our fantasy for miles

mountains bared their shoulder to the Sun
  the light surrounded us with glass
(our dance belongs in bright museums)
  a voice demanded *tickets into town!*
Colorado, you and me awakened slow
  stepping from a silver train to snow.

Outside small towns
the tree is always waiting
one arm extended heavy as my tongue,
the deputy
stares in electric waterfalls
twists a wristband
a few beerglass pirouettes,
his hands take time to tie their knot
dressed to marry
his silvered feet swing to the ground
he works for night's dark word
the crow,
the crow who asks: *are you alive?*

DAGUERROTYPE (Wyoming 1881)

Will Carver a vestpocket thumbdiver
his politico cheroot
flashed in the Wild Bunch
one hand (lightly) on Sundance.

Will Carver caught under a bowler hat
a cyclops glaring at the camera
the developed western outlaw
trapped as a boy in his mother's voice.

Sundance features throw shade
no one knows his eyes
posing a deadly cornerstone
fixing the Age to his balance
casually protecting the inventor of darkness.

CAVERNOUS MUSIC

Your gap toothed weariness

night's thundering gut
      thundering

  I drift its ravines

      and visit the deep
        the deep

turn you in

    to the law of each morning
    the law
      law

throw away my black shirts

keep our lathered horse
      horse
      horse

    Mister Death
    Mister Death
    Mister Death
    Mister Death

Billy carried green eyes
searching their tunnels
deeper than Mars
out where galaxies make clouds
he rode
the woman in space
becoming the whale
who spits bodies back :
Billy
infinity makes me crazy
let's run catch a train
my hands shake like gold in a well.

HANDCUFFS

You understand, I'm slow
it was just a touch
cops in leather coats
stylish revolvers
and then those fancy bracelets
metal getting warm on wrists
years sleeting by the window
dust of the solitude
crowded with loneliness
poems
with stripes on their arrival
a few joints
cops and robbers
bulletholes in the backseat
my body has been worn outside before
quick as silk pajamas
I write anywhere, die anywhere.

Some days collapsing
heavy enough
to throw bones on the ground
I drift with the man
who threw himself
from the tallest building
up there he could see
Earth has a crust
he longed to break through
the crowd
wanted him to fall
from the highest place
JUMP they said
JUMP THROUGH THE CEMENT
and when he came down
broken as a gallon of wine
people ran
to see his fists closing
and from their hands
I am falling
falling
miles through the salty grass.

THUNDERHEADS

Thunderheads bump the coast
flickering
flickering
owleyes of a miner
drink the sky from looming caves
a darkness
when firelight limbs
crack dry bones
each storm a song how we are thirsty.

Running from wounds
running in sweat
running in a crowd's rags
roar swollen arteries of the street
taking breath taking light
her hair broken open
my tongue drinking its scalp
rough rasp of the bull.

Summer takes us by the arms
brown, naked
morning of tremulous leaves
sleep creases
hair's magpie tangles
eye sap opening knots
shivering
where our roots must cross.

This night's moonslid blink
   feathery my gloom

     drumfingers shudder lamplight
   each vision

a sparrow upthrown
   breath crouched in its blood.

Earth commands life
our moonrise
razors between labor
to slit dark eyes
where earth lies dreaming
waters smoke
along air's dreamroads
algae stall
Reactors plumb the darkness
hone a ceaseless lance
piercing each bone.

KEEP YOUR HANDS IN SIGHT

Sucked by western sundowns west
how the image
melts for fleabit mirrors
Hollywood's chill fathering
slick dream reels melting into skin
the skin a gut-sewn tipi
torn by desperado dreams
the ritual's flint eye'd innocent
quicksilver hands, heroic movie hands.

There are places, California's
naked woman knew
these ridges long ago,
wind and rain, the bulldozer
scatters her remains
walking West
the fading Sun on our eyes
sometimes we hear her singing.

for Murietta

American all the way from England
    English all the way from Newcastle
    Geordie all the way from Ireland
      Irish all the way from Spain!
In Hermosillo, a woman watched
me singing down a dark ride south
a lute beside an oud
our emerging guitar's wildflung song
hands strumming visions
our deep eye's whisper
when history opens wide its arms
and Californians
return to mountains
laughing how they have always known.

The Author

PHILIP SUNTREE was born in England and now lives in Grass Valley, California. He is a maker of masks, carpenter, and teacher. His first book of poems, *The Stray Moon*, was published in 1975 by Turkey Press.

HIS WIFE SUSAN is also a poet and teacher. They have a son, Shannon, and a daughter, Califia.

The Book

FOUR HUNDRED copies of this book were hand-set in 14 point Bembo by Harry Reese, and printed by Sandra Liddell.

TWENTY-SIX copies have been hand-bound in boards by Sandra Liddell, lettered from A to Z, and signed by the author.